c h

animals observed

by
Brigitte Baumbusch

Stewart, Tabori & Chang

it may seem easy

The black-stone whale above was carved by Chumash Indians who lived in California. The eye is a shell.

These little animals are made of pleated rushes by the Anasazi. This people were the ancient inhabitants of the Grand Canyon in Arizona.

to make an animal

This group of stork-like birds was engraved on a rock in Tanzania (Africa) in ancient times. Prehistoric people all around the world made paintings or engravings on rocks, most of which depicted animals.

the first artists

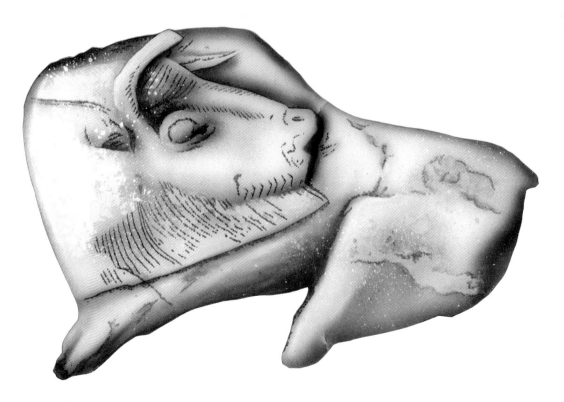

The bison above was carved from reindeer
horn more than 17,000 years ago.
At that time men still did not know how
to cultivate the fields, and they mostly
ate the meat from animals they had hunted.

made animals

People in the Stone Age sometimes painted the walls of entire caves with hundreds of animals. Those shown here were found in the caves of Lascaux in France.

This half-man, half-stag was depicted on a rock in another French cave. Perhaps he was really a witch-doctor dressed as an animal.

there are colorful animals

Here, a Japanese screen shows a group of splendid roosters with multicolored feathers.

This woodcut by M. C. Escher, a modern Dutch artist, is called *Sky and Water*. The white fish in the dark water gradually turn into black birds against a bright sky.

A woodcut is made by carving out from a block of wood the parts that are to remain white. The block is then coated with ink and pressed on a sheet of paper.

and black and white ones

some animals look good

This cat's name was Armellino and he had his portrait painted in the early nineteenth century. Behind him you can see a poem dedicated by the artist to the cat's mistress.

Albrecht Dürer, the German Renaissance artist who drew this rhinoceros more than four hundred years ago, had probably never seen one, just heard about them.

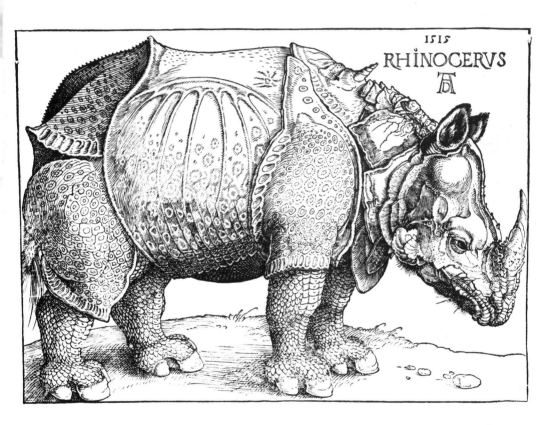

others are no beauties!

animals move

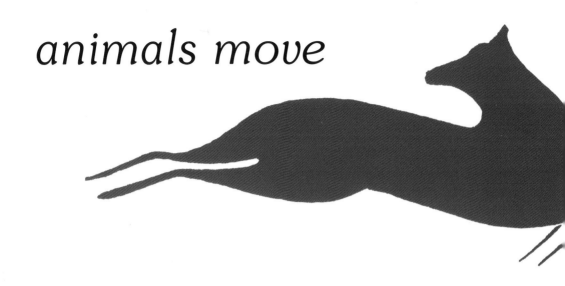

Above are racing gazelles from a prehistoric painting found on a rock in the Sahara desert in Africa, and at left is a little dog running on a leash, drawn in the early 1900s by Giacomo Balla, an Italian painter who enjoyed showing movement.

Below lies an ancient Chinese jade figurine
of a water buffalo resting with his keeper, a child.
In the Orient, water buffaloes are still used in the
same way that we
used to use
horses.

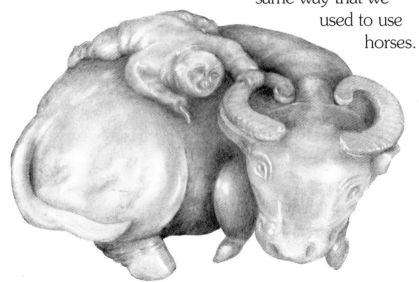

and rest

animals can be docile

A flock of sheep in single file turns home at the close of day. It was painted at the end of the nineteenth century by an Italian artist with the complicated name of Giuseppe Pellizza da Volpedo.

Cats, as we know, love to hunt. This cat with a bird in its mouth was painted by Pablo Picasso.

*... or
cruel*

animal babies have mothers

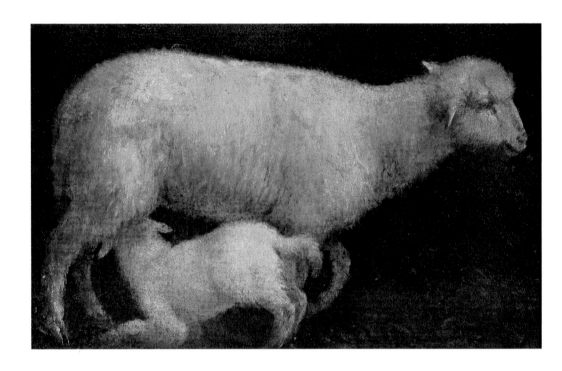

A mother sheep suckles her lamb. This was
painted in Italy about four hundred years ago
by an artist called Jacopo Bassano.

to take care of them

This beautiful example of medieval goldwork shows a hen taking her seven chicks for a walk.

A rhinoceros plays with her cub. This is a prehistoric rock engraving found in the Sahara. Today the Sahara is a desert, but thousands of years ago there were rivers and lakes, and so there were also many plants and animals.

and play with them

17

many animals work for us

The horse and the camel are animals that men have used to carry things for a long time in all parts of the world.

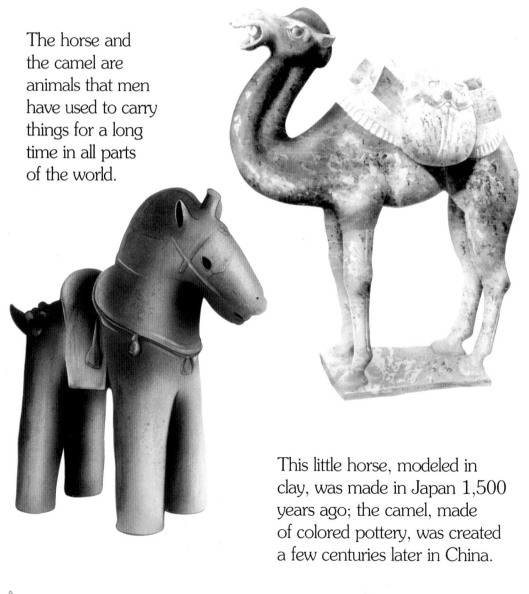

This little horse, modeled in clay, was made in Japan 1,500 years ago; the camel, made of colored pottery, was created a few centuries later in China.

Henri Matisse,
a French
painter, made
this painting
called
Goldfish
at the
beginning
of the
twentieth
century.
Goldfish
may not
be useful but
they're pretty
to look at.

or make our homes pretty

some are friends

Dogs and cats have always been the favorite pets of children. In the 1800s this American girl had her portrait painted together with her friends.

Snoopy is Charlie Brown's famous beagle friend.

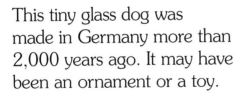

This tiny glass dog was made in Germany more than 2,000 years ago. It may have been an ornament or a toy.

and keep us company

21

there are fabulous animals

The unicorn is an animal that never existed. It was, however, often depicted during the Middle Ages as a gentle deer with a long horn growing from its forehead. This tapestry –a kind of carpet to hang on the wall– woven in France, shows one in an enclosure.

... of great charm

The little man with
a bird's head is one of
the odd creatures to be
found in paintings by
Hieronymus Bosch, who
lived in the Netherlands
five centuries ago.

... bizarre

Dragons never existed,
but were shown
as terrible serpents
or great
lizards
that
sometimes
breathed
fire. The one
shown here was
painted on a
Chinese porcelain
vase.

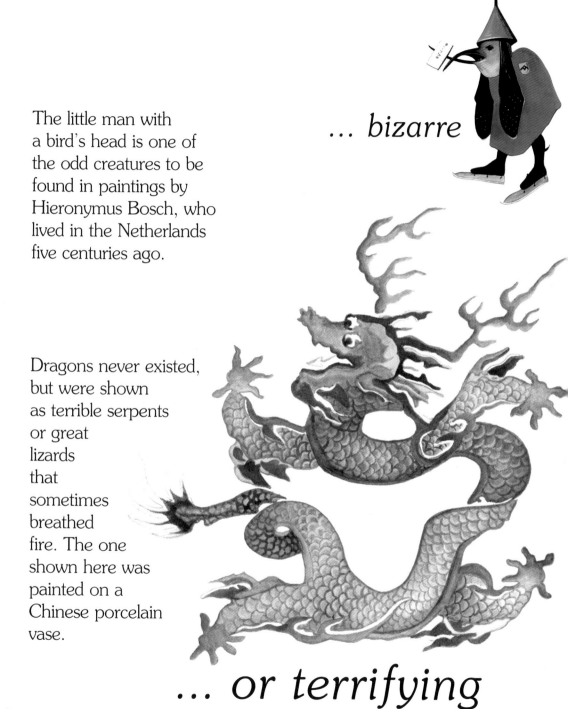

... or terrifying

sometimes animals

HHIACOLEOHII

This lion, the symbol of Saint Mark the evangelist, is painted on a page of a Gospel book, written by hand in Ireland during the Middle Ages.

The ancient Egyptians often depicted their gods in animal form. This bronze bird–an ibis–represents Thoth, god of wisdom and magic.

are used as symbols

The eagle has always been a symbol of power and for the Romans represented the rule of Rome in the world. The one shown here was carved on a medallion of colored stone in the time of the Roman Empire.

the animals most like us

Below, monkeys play cards as if they were real people. They were painted by David Teniers, an artist who lived in Flanders (today it's called Belgium) three hundred years ago.

At right, a seated
monkey in a Japanese
colored drawing.

are apes

Picture list

page 17
Hen with seven chicks in gilded silver. Medieval art of the 7th century. Monza, Cathedral Treasury. Drawing by Lorenzo Cecchi.

Engraving of a rhinoceros and its young. Prehistoric rock art, c. 8000 B.C. Tassili N'Ajjer (Algeria). After a copy by Henri Lhote. Drawing by Roberto Simoni.

page 18
Horse in full gear in terra cotta. Japanese art of the 5th century A.D. Tokyo, National Museum. Drawing by Lorenzo Cecchi.

Convoy camel in glazed terra cotta. Chinese art, T'ang dynasty, 8th-9th century A.D. Drawing by Ivan Stalio.

page 19
Henri Matisse (1869-1954): *The Goldfish*, 1911. Moscow, Pushkin Museum. Photo Scala Archives. © Succession Henri Matisse by SIAE, 1999.

page 20
Ammi Phillips (1788-1865): *Girl in Red with Dog and Cat*. New York, Museum of American Folk Art. Museum Photo.

page 21
Figurine of a dog in colored glass. Celtic art, 2nd century B.C., from Wallertheim, Palatinate Rhineland (Germany). Mainz, Mittelrheinisches Landesmuseum. Drawing by Lorenzo Cecchi.

The drawing of Snoopy from the comic strip "Peanuts" by Charles M. Schulz has been reproduced with the kind permission of Peanuts © United Feature Syndicate Inc.

page 22
The Unicorn in Captivity. French tapestry, c. 1500. New York, Metropolitan Museum of Art. Drawing Studio Stalio / Alessandro Cantucci.

page 23
Dragon, from a Chinese porcelain of the 15th century. Taipei, National Palace Museum. Drawing by Justine Thompson Bradley.

Hieronymus Bosch (1450-1516): Detail of the left wing of the *Temptation of Saint Anthony* triptych. Lisbon, National Museum of Ancient Art. Drawing by Lorenzo Cecchi.

page 24
Illuminated page from the *Echternach Gospels*. Medieval Irish art of the 7th century. Paris, Bibliothèque Nationale. Drawing by Ivan Stalio.

page 25
Bronze figurine of the god Thoth in the form of an ibis. Egyptian art, 5th century B.C. Turin, Egyptian Museum. Drawing by Lorenzo Cecchi.

Onyx cameo with the imperial eagle. Roman art, late 1st century B.C.-early 1st century A.D. Vienna, Kunsthistorisches Museum. Drawing Studio Stalio / Andrea Morandi.

page 26
David Teniers the Younger (1610-1690): *Monkeys Playing Cards*. Moscow, Pushkin Museum. Photo Scala Archives.

page 27
Drawing of a seated monkey. Japanese art, Edo period, 18th-19th century. Drawing Studio Stalio / Andrea Morandi.